CHAOS
UNDER MY
CALM

POEMS BY
ANJALI SINGH

INDIA • SINGAPORE • MALAYSIA

ISBN
Paperback 979-8-89446-603-3
Hardcase 979-8-89544-856-4

Dedicated to Mumma and Papa,

who gave me my first pen, paper and dose of encouragement.

Contents

Piled up	9
Flawed	11
Dreams	13
Anger	15
Misunderstood	17
How are you?	19
An open letter	21
3 AM Thoughts	22
To the guy down my street	24
Thoughts	28
Secrets	30
Within	31
Gaze	33
Suffocated	35
Pride	37
Somebody	39
Exhausted	40
Hollow	42
I'll wait for you	44

Setting free   46

Clouds   48

Tranquility   50

Memories   52

Darkness   53

Worth   55

Caged   57

Welcome to the 21st century   58

Hold on   60

Vindication   61

Drowning   63

Beyond you   65

Absolute Mess   66

Letting go   67

Fading away   69

The Right Thing   70

Where's Everyone?   72

Surrender to me   74

Perfection   77

Author's Note   79

Piled up

I still remember the first time I failed
It felt like the world ended
Like a mirror shattered and its pieces lost
It was an experience I had never prepared myself for
After all, recall the people you know who have failed
You only know their failures because they are successful now
Millions try and fail
Keep trying and keep failing
I didn't cry instantly

I remember the day you left
Without a sign, without a notice, without a tear
I sat in the alley all day
Didn't speak a word
Just kept sitting
I told myself, I didn't need to cry

I also remember the day when I was misunderstood
How could you not believe me
How could you not understand me
Do you even know me
Anger seeped in through my veins and filled my eyes
But I didn't let it flow,

How could I let it flow
The world did not want another weak person
It needed fighters, warriors, brave hearts
People who could defy the ordinary
Not people who cried all day
Social media told me that everyone's happy
And that I didn't really need to be so snappy

But every night, after the lights go off
After the world has dozed off
After the virtual screen darkens
It sparkles
It sparkles in the darkness
It slowly creeps from the side of the bed I have always avoided
It forms a cloud which I just cannot see through
A cloud which bursts bringing into reality all that I had piled
up
The pain, the sorrow, the anger, the guilt, the regret.
Sleep when it finally comes,
Makes sure to remind me of piling up emotions the next day
It tells me that the next night isn't going to be any different.
It tells me to wear my armor every day to bed
As the battle against the pile is a never-ending one.

Flawed

I was the apple of your eyes
The brightest star in your sky
For you, I was flawless
For you, I couldn't falter
But I did
I faltered, I fell, I had flaws
My lights have dimmed
And I have fallen not just once
But again, and again

You've still called me the apple of your eyes
To be honest, a dagger pierces my soul each time you do
I know you mean it
I know I am still the brightest star in your sky
But I know I have dimmed your sky
I have scraped your hopes
And I have flawed

Somedays, I wish you hated me
I wish you detested my presence
I wish you could say that I have been a disappointment
But you don't

Each "well-tried" of yours sinks my heart
And your endless love hurts boundlessly

I hope someday I rise
Rise from these ashes that I have burnt myself into
Rise enough to shine like the sun
I hope to take your hand
Walk you beyond these dim horizons
And show you how your trust has been well-placed
I hope someday, I can sit by the park
In the cheerful monotony
And reflect on my life
And look back at myself as neither flawed nor flawless.

Dreams

Lying down in bed
Gazing at the ceiling of my room
With books on my side
And dreams in my eyes
With so much to say
But only mute words that have chosen to stray
Stray in the fear of the void reflecting it back
Reflecting it to another void
Another void that will absorb it
And lose in its mayhem, a part of me

I turned sideways to accommodate more on the bed
I knew that dreams didn't lie alone
They came along with things I had to fit in
Struggles, the complimentary breakfast at the hotel I chose to
a trip to success.
Anxiety, my plus one to promenades of victory
And isolation, my closest companion

I close my eyes hoping to break free of the misery
I pull the blanket over to shield my solitude
If only escape plans were my forte

If only my armor was not a piece of clothing
And my source of tranquility so temporary.

I know my dreams are a facade
For they show me ecstasy and glee
They show me utopia and tell me it's viable
They motivate me to get up the next morning
Stuff my sack with the recipe for success
And head on to the promenade at the hotel with my closest
companion.

Anger

My anger's an earthquake
It parades unannounced
It might simmer down instantly
But it might also wreck lives

My anger's a broken glass
It shatters with a magnanimous voice
It hurts whoever comes to collect its pieces
And it repels all those in its vicinity

My anger's an upset child
It might cry a volume
It might scream all its complexities
But it will never be truly heard

My anger's a jailed innocent
It bangs itself against the bars at night
It cries during periods of solitude
But no one gets it, no one understands
It's been declared illegal
And it shall live like a curse

My anger's a part of me
A part of me that burns each time it's unveiled
A part of me that seeps in through the ashes
A part of me that brings out all the evil buried inside
Sometimes, it sounds like screams
Like arguments, like hatred
Other times, you can't hear it
It's crushed below pillows
Or streamed through the eyes
But my anger's still a part of me
And it always will be.

Misunderstood

Have you ever felt misunderstood?

I'll tell you how it feels

The core of your heart burns with anguish

Little volcanoes erupt in your soul

You fail to fathom your own emotions

Something crumbles inside you while you sit

Your only escape is your tears or your rage

Both of which you need to suppress

Both of which are condemned

The more you speak, the less you become of a girl

The less you become of an agreeable child or a congenial human

Simply because reasoning is neither accepted nor appreciated

Have you ever been the least preferred one?

I'll tell you how it feels

You begin by thinking it's funny

They obviously love you but don't show

Why do the rules change for others though?

Why is their inexpressible love expressed when it's not you?

Slowly, your smile starts to fade away,

And before you know it, the fun in funny vanishes
You still try and understand
Count your own flaws every night
Cry because they were the only people who were supposed to
love you despite your flaws
Slowly, you start accepting
It's like taking continuous little sips of hot water
Letting it burn your throat as it moves down slowly
You can feel your system accepting it.
It's like keeping your feet in cold water
Resisting it for the first few moments
And then not feeling a thing
It is like every other new thing
That your body eventually has to accept.

How are you?

They often ask me how I'm doing
But are they really asking
Will they sit with me and hear of the hurricanes within?
Do I be honest and tell them that some days are great
The sun shines as bright as my soul
And the wind makes me feel light
But there are other days as well
Days that don't shine as bright
Days that consume each ounce of my brightness
Days that leave me weak

Do I be open and tell them I've been feeling uneasy lately
Or will my spectrum of emotions frighten them?
And my range of display scare them away?
I cry too easily, I laugh too much, I hold too strong and I fall too harsh
I have so many people and I have no one
I have the best of things and the worst of things
I want to live a thousand lives but I don't know how to survive this one
Do I let my heart explode with all these thoughts or do I let it bleed internally?

Do I be curious and ask them if it's tough for them too?
Does life curse their happiness on some days?
Does it push them off and act like it doesn't care?
Do they have someone they share their miseries with?
And is their solitude a blessing or does it also turn into loneliness sometimes?

Or do I just pass a smile
Suppress the storm within and let them know
That I am fine.

An open letter

An open letter to all my "well-wishers"
No, a long skirt is not the correct advice
And no a saree doesn't make me look more wise
The cleavage that I displayed belongs to me
Just like the opinions that you pass on should be
And no tight jeans don't mean I want to be appealing
Maybe your sick orthodox mindset needs a bit of healing
There are days I lock myself in and wonder
If I am just a bundle of blunders
I wonder if you were actually right
And I let you into my sphere of happiness to only dim my inner light
But there are days like these, which come more frequently
When I let myself shine bright,
Brighter than you'd like
Bright enough to not only sparkle mine but many other's lives.
So dear, well-wisher...
In your well-ironed opinions, I'd like to put in a bit of crease
And request your benevolent beliefs to rest in peace.

3 AM Thoughts

There's something about 3:00 am
Something that takes away a part of our identity
Yet makes us more of ourselves

My recent 3:00 am tryst, however, was different
I was not thinking about my insecurities
Or about a reply to an argument I had
Not even about my material dilemmas
Or about the many issues of the world
I thought about death… Yes, death.

I was curious about this mystery called death.
I know death is as veracious as life
I know death is an inevitable reality

But does anyone really know death?

Does dying feel like dozing off to a long sleep to never wake
up again?
Does it fill one with the comfort of a mother's arms?
Or is it a void with no exits?

Does dying hurt?

Does it feel like a needle slowly piercing through the soul?

Or is it like a sudden splash of a water balloon?

Does the un-rushed decay feel like losing parts of oneself;

Does it hurt lying down there in helplessness?

Or is it just an emotionless ride of leaving behind remains of oneself?

Does time corrode our souls too?

Or does it leave it untouched in an attempt to preserve its piousness?

Is dying a turbulent take-off with no destination?

Or like a pleasant long drive to your favorite destination?

Is death a permanent exit from the cycle of life?

Or is it just a shift of our soul?

To a new beginning, a new chapter, a new story.

To the guy down my street

To the guy down my street

You are one of the first few people I see at sunrise

You are also one of the very few people who came but not left

You have been a constant

A constant in a world changing faster than time

There are days when you're missing

Missing, not gone.

You have been like the sun

Setting every evening only to rise again

I remember the first time you came to my place

I was at least a foot taller than you

And see, how you've matched up after all these years

Okay okay, you've become even taller

So, I remember the first time you came to my place

It was a Tuesday and I was in 9th grade, the age of a happy space

The sun had set, the heat had not

The garden was roaring with happiness

Happiness of the young kids laughing and playing

But you were here, at my doorstep

With the brightest smile I had ever seen
But what caught my attention were your eyes
The eyes which spoke a tale
A tale unheard, a tale unspoken, a tale unnoticed
You broke my stare with your voice
"Didi, istree ke liye kapde dene hain?"
I remember how I stood there with muted words
Not that I had been ignorant of the harsh realities
Not that I had never seen or heard about this
But because I was standing there,
Being a part of it.
I saw you again the next day while I was going to school
I remember how you hid your face on seeing me
How you buried the smile under the burden of the clothes you
carried
I spent the rest of the day preparing a questionnaire
I knew exactly what I had to ask you
The picture was pretty clear to me
This little boy was being tortured
He had been forced to work
He had been forced to quit education
He had been forced to fake a smile
He had certainly been forced.
And I was going to be your savior
Something I had always pictured myself being
So, I went home, all sorted and excited
Kept my eye on the door all day long

Only to know that you were not going to come that day
"Tuesdays and Fridays only"
My mother cleared my query
So, my questionnaire became longer
And my hopes higher
Well, it was Saturday already, and you hadn't shown up
"Sometimes, he doesn't come"
Mom was clearing my doubts again.
By Tuesday, I had a book of questions
But then it struck me,
What if the little boy was harmed
What if something unfortunate happened to him
I was your "to-be savior" after all, I had to take action
But on mom's insistence and weird reaction,
I decided to wait till Tuesday
I knew you were not going to come
I knew there was something wrong
I just knew
With false hopes and a heavy heart, I waited by the doorstep
But obviously, you were not going to come
Turns out, you did
That too with the same smile
Maybe a bit brighter this time (Probably because you had topped your class)
I stopped there yet again, with a blank stare and muted words
I could hear the voices of the kids playing in the garden
"Didi, istree ke liye kapde dene hain?"

I still remember that day

I will always remember that day

I understood how wrong I was

I understood how naive you were

I tried to understand why you were doing this

So, you did attend school

You were not being tortured

This was a choice, your choice

But I even understood things you didn't

I saw things that even you didn't

I saw how you didn't even know what you deserved

I saw you being okay with not getting to play

I saw you not complain about food or clothes

I saw you not want vacations

I saw you sacrifice happiness with a smile

The brightest smile I had ever seen

Many years have passed since then,

But you have been a constant

A constant in a world changing faster than time

I did not see you down the street today

I hope I never see you down the street again.

Thoughts

She ran across the knee-deep pasture,
the wild winds, the morning mist, the never-ending landscape
She let her hair flow free
Like the birds, she raced past
Like the air, she swiftly transited through
Like her mind which hosted millions of thoughts

She smiled for she recalled happy moments
The instant showed her the sun rising like hope in a summer
of darkness
The birds chirping in the vacuum of graving silence
The warmth of the cool mist in the dampness that could have
overtaken
The paramount stretch of nature and the infinite valleys
extending beyond view
Exuding vibrance just like her thoughts

The thoughts which now wandered off to moments of frustration
For the instant of the sun rising seemed unnecessary
The birds agitated for they took away her peace
The warmth of the cool mist seemed worthless in the light of
the sun

The infinite stretches symbolized superfluous moments
Her thoughts were an avoidable ocean on a cold winter evening

The thoughts that now crept towards sorrow
That instant the sun seemed like every other thing in life
Which came with a promise to last forever but was waived
away at will
The birds embodied the loud voices that have hushed her
existence
The warmth amidst the sun alluded to all the pretentiousness
she had encountered
And the incessant valleys dictated boundless dejection
Her thoughts, with each step, pushed her into pits of depression
Where she fell into her thoughts of struggle
Only to stand back to those of success

Halting round a tree,
She could see the web of thoughts that entangled her
And the unfolding of inevitable emotions it apportioned.

Secrets

In the corner of my heart
In its deepest vaults
Beyond access,
There are secrets
Secrets that will blow you apart
There's pain that will shatter you
And anger that will burn you
But the key to the lock is lost
Or maybe concealed

Some days when it's darker than usual
When the silence is eating me within
I wish to open the lock
And let my words burn kingdoms of pretense
Let my soul ignite all the dimming flames

But don't worry
I won't let the secrets out
I won't burn your mirage of pretense
I'll let myself soak in tears
I'll let my mind crumble with emotions
But I promise,
I promise I'll never give away the key.

Within

I look deep into the obscure cavity of your eyes
Eyes that are bewitched by never-ending spirals of thoughts
Surpassing the abyss of the greatest oceans
Thundering storms on the darkest nights
But I wish that was all

Gazing with all the profoundness I possess
I wish I knew there was nothing more
Nothing more than graves of memories buried ages ago.

But there's a shine in your eyes
A shine that blinds yet binds.
A shine that would surpass rainbows and crystal skies,
Brighten the darkest of rooms,
Extract the hollowest of cavities.

Perplexed, I delve deeper into the void
In the quest of finding myself in there
The hypnotic pursuit withdraws all restraints
And several struggles of revolt don't hold me back

My futile attempts smear relevant realizations
The mist makes me search for myself
Outside myself.
They won't tell me that the eyes are not mine
And that they'll never be.
The spirals, the abyss, the storms, the shine, the rainbows
All designs of a facade, a mirror that will invert my image
And show the externalities
A reflection that might sing mighty praises.
Or gracious venom drops
Yet be a pseudo portrayal built on modest models.

I'll wait for the fumes to evade,
For lucidity to flow in.
I'll wait till I escape my own confines of falsity
And realize that all I have ever pursued has been within me.

Gaze

I stand in the crowd beside you
I am sure I do
But why do their gazes weave another tale
Does my opacity shatter in the air that beholds it
Or is transparency the only view to an ordinary eye
Harsh moments tell me it's neither
They push me to the ground,
Entrap me through their words
And shove my anticipations till they lie beside me

Bruises, however, don't soften realizations
The best they can do is postpone them
Sometimes, postpone them until the pain mitigates
At others, till it elevates

The fictitious havoc of my storming brain
Patiently, in its calmness unwinds the curtains of falsehoods
The unclouded screen now displays images of designed ignorance
They whisper truths of deliberate malevolence
The whispers don't fade until I let them sink in
Until my soul accepts the inferiority the gazes offered
Until I accepted what was, just like it was

Every inch of my soul aches while I try to rise
I can now see through the moors of dampness
The sunshine beyond does not allude to me
But it propounds boundless hope
And what better has ever served humanity's existence?

Suffocated

Suffocation is a child of closed places
It seems to arrive at desperate times
When one is locked in a cupboard,
Trapped in a lift
Or Stuck in a small room.
It seems to arrive at desperate moments
When one is gasping for breath,
Stretching for space
Or Sweating till each ounce of water evaporates.

It's little known it's not a child to be restricted
Know it better and you'll find it everywhere
In the noisiest markets
In the busiest streets
In the most happening parties
Know it better and you'll find it in everyone
In the loud boy, you found annoying the other day
In the girl who seems to live the perfect life
In that cool person, you aspire to be

Its innocence will drag you down to dark alleys
Alleys you'd rather avoid visiting
But it won't leave your hand
Not until you succumb to its demands
Or leave.

Pride

I saw you looking around
With pride in your eyes
The stiffness of your posture
With the falsity that you've bred

I know you think you're above the sky,
Beyond the sea,
Larger than reality.
You think you're always right,
Rarely unpleasant,
Better than every other man,
You fabricate your stories,
Make yourself the hero,
And lead a pseudo-life every day.

But remember,
One day these shackles will break
Your self-made universe will explode
Every element of your falsity will see the grave
And when you look around
You'll find just yourself
No, you won't need a mirror

Or another entity
Every inch of your existence will scream its way out
And before long, you'll recognize yourself
You'll recognize yourself as the creator
The creator of your own destruction.

Somebody

Somebody, hold my hand and take me out
Out of this misery of an unsolved puzzle
Out of the dungeon with no light or life
Somebody, help me remove my soul
Because every part of me is mortified
And people say it's for no reason that can be specified
Somebody, push me off the tip
The tip hurts and there's nothing beyond it
The tip allures but there's nothing behind it
Somebody, come and hit me with the reality
For I have given everything to my dreams
And every bit of it scatters with all that I have believed in
Somebody, sit beside me and sing me to sleep
For my conscious mind is a maze of pain
With every turn unfolding a brighter aspect of darkness

Exhausted

There's no ounce of sweat on my forehead
No part of my body aches beyond control
My lips too shape in a crescent of happiness
And this is when you'll see it and you'll not
You'll be the closest and the farthest to me
You'll be the best and the worst judge of emotions
But it won't be your fault
It won't haunt you and follow you through the paths you take
It won't let awareness seep into you magically
And it truly won't be your fault
My exhaustion is a subset of a long weary ride
One you were not a part of
One that I myself am not sure of knowing too well
An unavoidable ride that has left me scarred
And no, the scars don't hurt
They remind me of the battle and the exhaustion
And they remind me that I survived it
And so, you'll never see me complaining about it
No, I am not a phenomenal survivor
Just a learner
A learner of the ways of life

Of the truth of exhaustion
And a simple fact
The fact that it's not just a part,
But a cause of who I am.

Hollow

There's a hollow in my life
And I am not sure what it is
There's a hollow in my life
And I've heard you whisper about it

There are moments in my life
When I feel I can tell exactly what it is
Maybe that missing dream,
that missing moment,
that missing person,
Or maybe my thoughts are not my own
It's a string entangled on my finger
The same string your whispers unleashed
Or is it a dream I saw last night
Which gifted glimpses of utopia
And made me feel incompetent to ever attain it
Or is it my time on the social media
Which weaves fairy tales and masters perfection
And makes me question every flaw I have ever had
Or is it you?
The reflection I see each morning,

Smiling back at me with hushed tones
Hiding layers beneath to save me from the storm,
And whispering tales to perplex life's austerity.

I'll wait for you

When the gloomy winter evening takes over
When your arrival is just an insane idea
When hopes have left each heart they lodged in
I'll wait for you
I'll try to look beyond the mist
I'll keep the curtains apart all day
I'll not let myself fall prey to the pessimism around me
For I know your shine is inevitable
Sometimes, you delay but you never deny
And that is why I'll wait for you

Even when I am stuck in a desert of disapproval
When your presence is compared to a mirage
I won't let go of my hopes
I'll run to each mirage
For I know even if I don't find you a 100 times
You'll be there somewhere
Finding me in other places
And if this is destiny's test, I know we'll succeed
For even if you take a lifetime,
I'll wait for you.

I'll wait for you like a child lost in the midst of the city

I'll cry my heart out

But I won't bury my belief

I won't let the city lights blind me

Or the incessant noises mislead me

I'll look around in each direction

For I know you'll be arriving from one

And I will, always, wait for you.

Setting free

My vision seems blurred today
I think it's filled with rage
My eyes are an ocean
I think it's the tears
My cheeks feel warm
I think it's the embarrassment

I sit in a corner and cry
Beg you to stop
Tell you I am trying
But are you listening?
You told me I stink of betrayal
You told me that I was a zero
And you kept repeating
Repeating till each spectrum of my confidence exploded

You forgot all the moments I have spent crying
All the moments I kept trying
You told me results won't matter
Not if I worked hard enough
Not if I showed passion

And I did, I tried, I persevered
But you have been sly
You have been smart
And you have been a liar.
Each morning I look at you
And I see you look back at me
I see the disappointment in your eyes
Your screams at my failures haunt me each night
Your impatience towards me increases with time
And your hatred towards me gets unbearable with each passing
moment.
And I try very hard to set you free
Free from miseries, free from the pain, free from me
But is it ever possible to set one free from oneself?

Clouds

As a child, a bird was all I wished to be

To fly across the sky and over the sea

But lately, it doesn't intrigue me as much

I guess the indolence of flying so long makes me lose the clutch

Or maybe being a bird never intrigued me

The sea or the sky or the idea of freedom the actual interest might be

So one evening, when I sat on my balcony

I gazed at the sky which absurdly seemed uncanny

The clouds had a definite formation

I could say they were trying to pass on information

But I was not sure what or why

Only if the message was automatically dropped by

But I kept gazing

There was one particular group of clouds that I kept chasing

They lit up the sky like a candle lights up a dark room

It was as if Picasso was up in heaven trying to erase Earth's gloom

It seemed like the almighty had no task so they picked up this one

The task of painting the sky might have seemed remarkably fun

The clouds for me are much more than just tiny droplets
gathered together
The clouds for me are an indication of the best weather
They are an art of the purest kind
They are a connection undefined in humankind
Their last moments are an example of the most altruistic cases
As they shower love in the form of sprinkles and bring smiles
on uncountable faces
So, every time I see a sky filled with clouds
I keep gazing till they decide to enshroud
It feels like an indication from eternity
Visually displaying how even the mildest of things can be so
pretty.

Tranquility

My brain doesn't rest
It's stuck in traffic
It's lost in a maze
It's hurt by thoughts
My head spins
I have lost too much
I have gained too little
I try to ingrain positivity
I try to keep my calm
I try to filter my thoughts

But I am being followed by shadows
They wait till I reach the narrow lane
They scare me with the reality
They push my thoughts back a thousand miles
And the journey of pain is revised.

My miseries have been my lovers
My miseries have been my destructors
And my head has been a home to them
And to all that I have ever been acquainted with

Finding peace in sleep has been redundant
For my dreams transform into narrow lanes

But one day, when my soul is tired
I hope my brain gives in
I hope it loses this battle against itself
And kneels down to tranquility.

Memories

Today your memories revisited
They no longer bring that sparkle in my eyes
They no longer brighten up my face with a crescent
Today your memories metamorphosed
They pricked something inside me
They filled my eyes like an empty well
Today your memories haunted
And I wish I could just leave every time they are recited
My cheeks hurt from the force I lift them with
My brain brings to life, instances buried away
And the havoc awaits my destruction while I sit there with a plain face

No, I don't have anything against you
And no, I don't hate you
You'll always be the best, you'll always be loved
But your memories are a trip I'd rather avoid
For they will always be a reminder
A reminder of all that I could not be.

Darkness

I met you in the fall of '17
You stood there with a wide smile
Took my hand into yours
My gaze fixated on you
And all that I could see was you
I didn't watch out for the pebbles in my path
I didn't look out for the directions you took
I surrendered myself to you
And you led me to the darkness
I have still hoped for light
For good days, for sanity
And I won't lie, I've had some of those
But I won't lie, they were balanced out
For the burden of the darkness weighed far more
For my eyes are streams of river and my heart is a yard of pain
And you, my reflection, are my biggest fear
I have started hating you
And then I have hated myself for the hatred I have gathered
I have questioned myself way too often
And I have hurt myself even more
But this tunnel of darkness doesn't seem to end
And your grasp is too strong

Maybe, I too don't want to let go
But the cracks in my existence torment me
And my willingness to proceed plagues me
And questions wreak havoc in my head
For I don't know whom to ask
I don't even know if there's an answer
But some days, my mind loses control
And my heart cries out for answers
Are you there? Are you listening?
For my mind and heart race in a battle
And either's victory is my loss
My tears gather in moments of desolation
And questions drop out in the void
My hand is still in yours and your eyes away from me
You seem like a different person now and I see scars
Are these battle scars or marks of surrender?
Are you a part of me or a part of my destruction?
And is this darkness a temporary tunnel or my unrealized
reality?

Worth

I have been standing steady in the rain
For my worth is greater than a few drops
I have been standing unbent in the wind
For my worth is higher than a few particles
I have been racing with every car on the street
For my worth is pushing me beyond sanity

I have been trying to prove myself each day
I have been trying to show them I am capable
To make them see how I can do it
To tell them my worth
And with every passing moment
The rains get heavier, the winds harsher and the cars faster
But my plea for recognition does not fade
I drive myself into fiercer paths
For they might see me then
But somehow, they don't

And with every passing night sleep gets harder to catch
It's even harder to let go of it
For my sleep is an escape
To a world with no masters

To a place where I can hide from even myself
Bury my thoughts and let my pain suppress in ignorance

The passing time pierces holes in my existence
And I compete for the pettiest things
For my worth might arise from something
And maybe then, they'll see it
They'll know and understand me
And all my efforts won't be futile

My brain traces different paths though
I wish I could control it like it controls me
It's been sabotaging my existence
And stabbing through my purpose
For it's been asking me who they are
And if it matters what they think

Caged

Am I lost in my reflections,
Or am I caught in the restrictions
Am I too shy,
Or am I not allowed to fly
Am I too small to have a say,
Or am I being suppressed bit by bit every day
Am I to stay this way all my life,
Or am I allowed to go out and strive
Is freedom just another word in the dictionary,
Or is everything I do really unwary
Are they always correct,
Or am I too naive to suspect
Does there actually exist a book of rules,
Or are they using it as one of their oppressing tools
Every day, I hope for something good,
But nothing my friend lifts my mood
So, is it justified for me to be outraged?
Or will I spend my life being caged?

Welcome to the 21st century

Welcome to the 21st century,

The age of millennials

The fast-paced life

The period where everyone's aware yet unaware

Meet mankind's most ambitious self

See them race through their days

See them not blinking in fear of losing the moment

See them trying to be the best

But wait, don't stop for long in your quest

Or you'll fall behind, way behind

Welcome to the new way of life

The rollercoaster you climbed for the thrill

The rollercoaster which lasts more than 5 minutes

The rollercoaster that stops getting fun

Welcome to the blues

And observe those empty, sad faces in the metro that don't look around

The eyes of the poor kid right in front of that metro station

The upset soul through the exuberance of the most buoyant
people
Notice contentment losing its grip on each individual you've
known
The shadow of depression covering the rays of happiness

Welcome to the hollow
The hollow that shut its door and caged every being it ever
consumed
The hollow that innocently closes its fists tightly around your
fingers
The hollow that is slowly victimizing the world
And is the mirage you went running for in a desert of oblivion

Hold on

One day despair shall leave each heart it lodged in
One day gloom shall evade each soul it seeped in
Heavy hearts will weigh out their miseries
Agonizing appearances will heave sighs of relief
But until then, hold on
Hold on to the despair and the gloom
To the miseries and the agony
They, like all things, shall scar
But like all things, they'll pass

Today, the night might seem long
And the wait for the day prolonged
The winter might get incessantly freezing
And this interminable expectation for warmth disillusioning
The tsunami might seem to be taking over
And even the last ray of hope to live might have disappeared
But in these moments of lost hopes and darkness, hold on
Even when it unveils its ugliest facet
And brims you with torment
Let it test you, let it see what you're made of
For your patience will pay off and the day shall arrive
And with it shall arrive warmth and the lost hope of life
But until then, my friend, hold on.

Vindication

I've gulped it down my throat
And locked it in myself
I am sure I have seen it before
But I am not prepared
Yes, I could see it heading towards me
Its volume scares me out of my wits
It's speed dreads me out of sleep
But I am standing still, like always
And like always, it's not out of bravery or undying strength
My hushed existence has known words don't help
And how temporary an attempt to escape would be.

Entrapped in this turmoil,
I let it enter inside me
I let it haunt my own soul
I can feel it moving down my throat
And quenching all the optimism I bred
Something tells me my crime must have been severe
For the pain needs to be justified
And all these unwarranted emotions need to halt
For right now, they are storming inside me

Pacing each time with a bigger magnitude
And shattering all in its wake
Whatever I say or do doesn't seem right
For even a thousand prisoned nights later
Their judgments have not announced my vindication.

Drowning

I am gasping for breath
My eyes are closed
My head's underwater and my body's afloat

I keep drowning by the second
But sorrow doesn't take me into its arms
It's hope that does, a funny hope
A hope that the depth of this ocean will be my bed
That its surface won't scratch my wounds
Its silence will let me be
And its acceptance won't dictate its rules upon me

My gasps for breath tone down to a surrender
A peaceful surrender
In an ocean of water, I can feel some on my face
It's close to the corners of my eyes
It's not pain I know
For then, it would have been familiar
It's relief, that once floated
That once soared high in the sky
And raced past oceans

Oceans, the depths of which seemed intriguing
And now the depths of which were my cradle of peace

My eyes open and see the void around
There was a time this haunted sight would make me want to vanish
Or shut my eyes and hope to wake up from this horror
But in this moment, they stayed open
They stayed for the void didn't hurt them
There was a calm in the absence of everything they ever knew
Looking up, a few distant hands came into their sight
But my hands didn't stretch
For the help seemed a facade
And the world below my only escape

So I let go,
And now with no gasps for breath,
Eyes wide open
My entire existence underwater
And a faint realisation of something like a smile on my face

I can see myself drowning.

Beyond you

While crossing smiling faces on empty streets
Do their layers of pretense haunt you back home?
Does the sorrow of the girl down the street snatch your sleep?
Does the young boy's acceptance of torment wreck your conscience?
Did the muted screams come past those walls today?
Those walls of the most sophisticated, the most reputed
Does their arrival ring a bell?
A familiar one perhaps.

While a million hearts break every day
Does the ache of every heart, break you down?
Or does your heartbreak make the loudest sound?
Each broken soul is not for you to mend
But did you let your sorrow dig graves of empathy?
For your mirror shattered closest to you
But there are mirrors broken beyond your ambit
The voices of which were hushed before they were heard
And the cries of which were lost in the mayhem

Absolute Mess

This might be the happiest I have ever been
A few drops evade my eyes at night though
This might be the most freedom I have ever had
My head rests on my own arms at sunsets though

There's an emptiness that hurts
There's a wound that's fresh
There are other wounds too
Some healing, some leaving scars, some inexplicable

Then there are reminders of all that I am not
All that I never was, and can never be
My heart sinks as they're right
But is it all that I am?
Is it all that counts?

I pose questions to kindle positivity
I try to look at it as a balancing act of life
I look at all that I have
But am I finding lights in a tunnel?
And is this all my attempt to romanticize an absolute mess?

Letting go

There will always be nights one can't forget
This one was special and well, dramatic
There will always be moments you doubt if they really even
existed
And I would have thought that it was all a dream
Or better yet, a nightmare
But it wasn't and so I lay here with a bunch of memories
And a scarred heart, and a mind hosting a million thoughts

Well, you looked just fine and you felt fine
There was something about you that I couldn't explain
Probably still can't
There was something about you that made me fall for you
It made me fall for something I saw the end of
But it all felt so right
And in that moment, I didn't want to be cautious
In that moment, I wanted to live a hundred lives
And in that moment, I dropped all my walls of surveillance

But the morning sun brings in too much light
It seeps in the reality through my front door
We weren't a match

And we never could be
It was all crystal clear to my brain
Voices resounded with reality
For you were not the one for me and I was not the one for you
But my heart hadn't learned to let go
It embraced the torture of finding hope in a dungeon
But it did not want to let go
It forced my sleep to evade due to the terror of nightmares
It crushed my self-respect like I could have never imagined
And it vanquished my peace like I didn't deserve it
But it still didn't allow me to let go
How could I even blame it though?
It felt those feelings for the first time
It didn't even keep expectations
It gloated in the little moments of happiness
And soon, it valued the space more than you
And that is when it didn't have feelings left for you

There are nights that one always wants to remember
And this was one that I'd revise to bed every night
For it took an ocean of courage for me to let go
And I did, I finally did.
With tears in my eyes, and a heart heavier than ever before,
I let go.
And even when it felt like something crumbled inside me a
million times,
I held myself and let go.

Fading away

You can try to hold on
Hold on to the shiny side of things
The greener side of the grass
The rainbows on a rainy day
But one day
When you've held your ground for long
And you close your eyes for a second
A second of tranquility, of peace
A second that you thought you deserved after years of holding on
That one second will change it all
And you would see how fickle it all was
The shiny side, the green grass, the rainbow
All fading away almost instantly
Voices in your head will tell you that it's you
They will blame you for your insincerity
For your selfish second.
And while you're left in the rain alone

Away from the badger,
Close your eyes
Let your tears camouflage
And let go

The Right Thing

How long do you push?
Till when do you drag?
Because I have been pushing my feelings and dragging them around
And some nights, I see myself brimming with emotions
I see the tipping point and I hold myself as tight as I can
For I don't want to fall
I don't want to let the right thing bring me down

But don't get me wrong
There are so many parts of you that I treasure beyond measure
You've been my light in the darkest times
And a ray of sun on dull, cloudy days
You're the most wonderful I've known
But there are parts of you that hurt
And there are parts of you that tell me that our future's a blur
It's a mirage in a desert
It's beautiful from a distance but does it even exist?
And I am not naive
For I know what I should do
But I can't let the right thing tear me apart

Some days I wonder
I wonder if I am delaying the pain or amplifying it
I wonder if I am fooling you or myself
You've been so kind to me
So kind that the idea of hurting you hurts me
But will time really fix everything?
Will it amend you or my hopes?
Will the thorns in your roses never prick my heart?
There are also days when I wonder if I am just a coward
Am I simply scared of breaking my own heart one more time?
Or am I scared of being alone?
These thoughts keep running through my mind
But nothing convinces me to do the right thing

There are a few things I wanted to know
Would you have opened your heart to me and unveiled all the
layers?
Would you have changed for me?
Would you have loved me like I wanted you to?
Or maybe, don't tell me
I don't want hope to weaken me down
I don't want expectations to create pseudo-realities
I don't want dismay to drown me again
Maybe these questions are better left unanswered
Because maybe then, I'll finally do the right thing.

Where's Everyone?

It's consuming me
I can feel its hands around my neck
It seduces me till I let down my shield
It plays with me for a second there
And the next second it's not a game
It slowly takes a grasp in there
And I notice losing my breath
Then suddenly I am out of breath
And no the grasp doesn't let me go
I am gasping for air that isn't there
My silent screams awake none
My family away, probably asleep
Unaware of my misery
My friends away, maybe awake
Engulfed in their own misery

I try again to set me free
But the grasp gets stronger and stronger
And I see myself battling
I can feel tears on my face though
Is it my rage or helplessness?

I can feel the world swiftly fading away

Can no one else see the tears? The rage? The struggle?Is it all in my head?

Has my soul abandoned already

And is my mind fighting these battles?

Where's everyone?

Why can't they feel what I feel?

Why can't they feel this pain, this misery?

Why can't they lend a helping hand?

My eyes are closing as I wrestle

And darkness is taking over

I still don't see a help in sight

And now it's all black as the night

Black as a void I had never experienced

It's quiet too

It's almost calm

It's almost peaceful

There's no struggle to breathe

There's no hope of help

There's no pain of losing

There's absolutely nothing

So have I lost all the pain in the world or have I lost the world?

Surrender to me

I have been closing the gates
For you, yourself are unaware of what your arrival states
I have been closing the curtains
As the winds may convey to you how this place burdens
I have been blocking each exit
And your entrance will mark this sphere as everywhere you
can exist

Hello, welcome to my world
Relish your excitement on the entrance before it is hurled
Your eyes exhibit an alteration as you look aghast at the mess
What you're looking at are forbidden pieces of distress

Stop! Please don't take a seat
You might want to remain on your feet
For my world changes like the weather
And your comfort in here might entangle you forever
I can see your eyes set on the trunk
Don't mistake it with an irresponsibly placed junk
If you look around and close enough
Figuring out many more trunks won't be tough
Some of these might be old

Their antiquity might allure you into considering them gold
Some of these trunks fall closer chronologically
And even your wisest guesses won't answer accurately

Your gaze at me seeks explanations and presents a bundle of
notions
Well, these trunks are my boxes of emotions
The roots of which lie beyond my sightlines
I am certain they spread across different timelines
Their distinctions pave way for a path they all have in common
Each path has led to their burial in my world where they have
befallen

I can see you've taken a seat in my little tent
You've inevitably dodged all warnings that I have constantly
sent
I don't blame you for in me you've placed a belief
And you didn't have any means to figure out any deceit

Close your eyes my friend, and surrender yourself to me
I will take you down a path to the place you're meant to be
You'll remain safe in my extravagant trunk
And don't worry, I'll never let you be confused with junk
Your exit here will be a part of your distant dreams
You'll remain in there regardless of how loud your silence
screams
However, you will find answers to a lot of your questions

My only hope is with these responses, your suffocation lessens
Those trunks contain emotions that I have left unexpressed
And your entrance was your nod to living a life being suppressed.

Perfection

Her life was under her subjection,
All she sought was perfection.
But does perfection exist?
Or is it just another myth?
Oblivious to life's verity,
She sailed with utmost sincerity.
Everyday was an inception
To something which would lead her to perfection.
She did make mild mistakes,
But they were too mild to agitate.
Then one day these few mistakes cluttered,
And something new for her fluttered.
Perfection was actually a myth,
It truly did not exist.
The truth was hard to digest
She was all the more distressed.
She felt that happiness would never find her door
And she'll be happy no more.
But she proved herself wrong,
And she came out of it strong.
She had a smile on her face
Which spoke volumes of her state
Perfection was actually a myth
But it didn't really need to exist.

Author's Note

For the longest time I remember, I have always liked writing. Whether it was a dear diary account of a tough day or an "I love you, Mom" poem, I have found solace in the rhythm of words flowing down on a piece of paper. I was around 18 when I started storing the poems that I wrote. The intent was never to publish them. In fact, I hid most of my poems from everyone I knew. There was an unexplained fear of being misconstrued or letting someone inside, letting them peek into my soul and into my deepest thoughts.

However, with age, the boundaries extended, and I let my close ones in. This book, dear reader, is a piece of my heart. You must have felt some or all of these emotions at one point or the other. I have taken a deep dive into them and laid them out for you. While they might have been drawn out from scoops of my life, I now hand them to you to give them your own flavor.

A special note of gratitude to Bhai, Bhabhi, Esha, Nishtha, and Ritweek for their encouragement and support in publishing this book.